Handy Mississippi Genealogy Handbook

by Gary L. Morris

©2015 Gary L. Morris

ISBN-13: 978-1506183084

ISBN-10: 1506183085

Table of Contents

Notes

Genealogical Research in Mississippi

There are many genealogical records and resources available for tracing your family history in Mississippi. Because there are so many records held at many different locations, tracking down the records for your ancestor can be an ominous task. Don't worry though, we know just where they are, and we'll show you which records you'll need, while helping you to understand:

1. What they are
2. Where to find them
3. How to use them

These records can be found both online and off, so we'll introduce you to online websites, indexes and databases, as well as brick-and-mortar repositories and other institutions that will help with your research in Mississippi. So that you will have a more comprehensive understanding of these records, we have provided a brief history of the "Magnolia State" to illustrate what type of records may have been generated during specific time periods. That information will assist you in pinpointing times and locations on which to focus the search for your Mississippi ancestors and their records.

A Brief History of Mississippi

There were approximately 30,000 Native American Indians of various tribes living in what we now call Mississippi when the first Europeans arrived in the early 16th century. By the time the French had settled the area in 1699 however, only the three largest tribes remained, the Chickasaw, Choctaw, and Natchez. The Natchez were eventually wiped out by the French between 1729 and 1730 in retaliation to the massacre of a colony of French settlers on the Natchez Bluffs.

Hernando de Soto was the most notable of the Spanish explorers who ventured into the area. He arrived between 1540 and 1541 seeking mineral wealth. Upon finding none, the Spanish lost interest in the area and the French established a settlement at Biloxi Bay in 1699. The French soon established settlements at Mobile in 1702, Natchez in 1716, and New Orleans in 1718. Spain once again took control of the region after the French lost the French and Indian War, but ceded the area east of the Mississippi to England.

The Spanish continued to rule the area until 1795, but maintained a garrison there for another three years. Mississippi was organized as a territory in 1798, and for the next 9 years grew enormously in population. Mississippi was granted statehood on December 10, 1817 and exemplified the American frontier until the outbreak of Civil War.

In three treaties between 1820 and 1832, the remaining Indian tribes signed over their land to the United States. The availability of these fertile lands led to boom of cotton agriculture and slavery sweeping across the state. As slavery increased, so did profits, and the Mississippians who benefited began to justify slavery morally, socially and economically. The plantation owners of Mississippi grew to believe that no price was too high to pay to maintain slavery, even secession and civil war.

So intent was the state on maintaining slavery that it became to second state to cede from the union on January 9, 1861. Because of the strategic importance off the Mississippi River, the area occupied a central place in Union strategy. As such, much of the fighting during the Civil War took place in Mississippi, the most concentrated Union attack coming at Vicksburg, which eventually proved a turning point in the war in favor of the Union. Of the 78,000 men from Mississippi who fought for the Confederacy, close to 30,000 lost their lives.

The Reconstruction era was a tumultuous time for Mississippi; Republicans and Democrats clashing over the rights of newly free African Americans. While the Republicans encouraged blacks to get involved in the political system by voting and running for office, the Democrats resisted full freedom with all their might. The confrontation lasted until 1875 when Democrats, using violence and intimidation wrested control of the state from the Republicans.

Blacks in Mississippi were pushed back into slavery in everyway except name, and segregation laws and a new state constitution in 1890 completely usurped their rights. White political solidarity lasted from the Reconstruction era right into the 1960's and according to the Tuskegee Institute, an educational institute for blacks that opened in 1888, 538 blacks were lynched in Mississippi between 1883 and 1959.

Important Dates in Mississippi History

1699– French settlement established at Biloxi

1763 – Ceded from France to Great Britain

1781 – Part of Mississippi ceded to Spain

1783 – Most of Mississippi claimed by Georgia

1795 – U.S. receives all of Mississippi west of Florida in Pinckney treaty

1796 – U.S. takes control of area claimed by Georgia

1798 – Organized as a separate territory

1802 – Georgia relinquishes claims to the area

1817 – Statehood

1831 – Choctaw and Chickasaw Indians removed

1861 – Secedes from Union

1863 – Battle of Vicksburg

1870 – Readmitted to Union

Famous Battles Fought in Mississippi

Many battles took place in Mississippi during the Civil War, and the **Civil War Academy** has excellent accounts of them all, providing; locations, dates, names of Commanders, names of Units involved, and number of casualties.

These battle accounts that exist can be very effective in uncovering the military records of your ancestor. They can tell you what regiments fought in which battles, and often include the names and ranks of many officers and enlisted men.

Civil War Academy: http://www.civilwaracademy.com/civil-war-battles-in-mississippi.html

Common Mississippi Genealogical Issues and Resources to Overcome Them

Boundary Changes: Boundary changes are a common obstacle when researching Mississippi ancestors. You could be searching for an ancestor's record in one county when in fact it is stored in a different one due to historical county boundary changes.

The **Atlas of Historical County Boundaries** can help you to overcome that problem. It provides a chronological listing of every boundary change that has occurred in the history of Mississippi.

Atlas of Historical County Boundaries:
http://publications.newberry.org/ahcbp/documents/MS_Consolidated _Chronology.htm#Consolidated_Chronology

Name Changes: Surname changes, variations, and misspellings can complicate genealogical research. It is important to check all spelling variations. Soundex, a program that indexes names by sound, is a useful first step, but you can't rely on it completely as some name variations result in different Soundex codes. The surnames could be different, but the first name may be different too. You can also find records filed under initials, middle names, and nicknames as well, so you will need to **get creative with surname variations** and spellings in order to cover all the possibilities. For help with surname variations read our instructional article on **How to Use Soundex**.

get creative with surname variations:
http://obituarieshelp.org/blog/?p=634

How to Use Soundex link to: http://obituarieshelp.org/blog/?p=505

Mississippi Genealogical Organizations and Archives

Genealogical resources include not only records, but the organizations that house them, or can direct you to them. These institutions include: *Archives, Libraries, Genealogical Societies, Family History Centers, Universities, Churches, and Museums.*

Following are links to their websites, their physical addresses, and a summary of the records you can find there.

Archives and Libraries

Mississippi Archives - Birth and Death Records, Census Records, County Records, Court Cases, Dawes Rolls, Enumeration of Educable Children, Freedmen's Bureau Labor Contracts, Marriage Records, Military Resources

William F. Winter Archives and History Building
200 North St.
Jackson, MS 39201
Tel: 601-576-6876
Fax: 601-576-6964

Mailing Address:

P.O. Box 571
Jackson, MS 39205-0571

Mississippi Archives:
http://mdah.state.ms.us/arrec/gen_research.php

National Archives Southeast Region (Atlanta) – slave sales records, WWI draft registrations, civil rights records, civil war records, and more

5780 Jonesboro Road
Morrow, GA 30260
Phone: (770) 968-2100
Fax: (770) 968-2547

National Archives Southeast Region (Atlanta):
http://www.archives.gov/atlanta/exhibit/index.php

Mississippi State University – wide variety of resources especially for genealogical research; especially valuable is the manuscript collection

Special Collections-Genealogical Library
P.O. Box 5408
Mississippi State, MS 39762
Phone: (601) 325-7679
Fax: (601) 325-3560

Mississippi State University:
http://library.msstate.edu/specialcollections

Mississippi Genealogical and Historical Societies

Genealogical and historical societies have access to extensive catalogues of genealogical data. They are also able to offer expert guidance for genealogical researchers. Many members are professional genealogists who are most willing to share their expertise in finding ancestors.

Mississippi Genealogical Society – wide variety of genealogical resources including family histories, cemetery, and bible records

P. O. Box 5301
Jackson MS 39296
Tel.: 601.613.2620
Email: Info@MSGenSociety.org

Mississippi Genealogical Society:
http://www.msgensociety.org/index.html

The **Mississippi Department of Archives and History** has a listing for many smaller **County Genealogical Societies**

County Genealogical Societies:
http://mdah.state.ms.us/admin/fmhslst.html

Mississippi Mailing Lists

Mailing lists are internet based facilities that use email to distribute a single message to all who subscribe to it. When information on a particular surname, new records, or any other important genealogy information related to the mailing list topic becomes available, the subscribers are alerted to it. Joining a mailing list is an excellent way to stay up to date on Mississippi genealogy research topics. Rootsweb have an extensive listing of **Mississippi Mailing Lists** on a variety of topics.

Mississippi Mailing Lists link to:
http://lists.rootsweb.ancestry.com/index/usa/MS/misc.html

Mississippi Message Boards

A message board is another internet based facility where people can post questions about a specific genealogy topic and have it answered by other genealogists. If you have questions about a surname, record type, or research topic, you can post your question and other researchers and genealogists will help you with the answer. Be sure to check back regularly, as the answers are not emailed to you. The Mississippi Message Boards at **Rootsweb** are completely free to use.

Rootsweb:
http://boards.rootsweb.com/localities.northam.usa.states/mb.ashx

Mississippi Newspapers and Periodicals

Many genealogy periodicals and historical newspapers contain reprinted copies of family genealogies, transcripts of family Bible records, information about local records and archives, census indexes, church records, queries, land records, obituaries, court records, cemetery records, and wills. The following sites have historical Mississippi newspapers and periodicals that you can search online or on-site.

GenealogyBank.com – free searchable database of Mississippi newspaper archives, 1818–1964

GenealogyBank.com:
http://www.genealogybank.com/gbnk/newspapers/explore/USA/Mississippi/

Library of Congress Digital Newspaper Directory – free searchable database of historical U.S. newspapers dating from 1690-present

Library of Congress Digital Newspaper Directory:
http://chroniclingamerica.loc.gov/search/titles/

The Online Books Page – links to historical Mississippi books and periodicals available for viewing online, dating from mid-16th century

The Online Books Page:
http://onlinebooks.library.upenn.edu/webbin/book//browse?type=lcsubc&key=Mississippi%20--%20History%20--%20Periodicals

NewspaperArchive.com – largest online database of historical newspapers in the world.

NewspaperArchive.com: http://newspaperarchive.com/

Historical Mississippi Maps and Gazetteers

Maps are an integral part of genealogical research. They help us to locate landmarks, towns, cities, parishes, states, provinces, waterways and roads and streets. They also help us to determine when and where boundary changes might have taken place, and give us a visualization of the area we're researching in.

For locating place names, a gazetteer is the best possible resource for any genealogist. Gazetteers are also sometimes called "place name dictionaries", and can help you to locate the area in which you need to conduct research. Below are links to the maps and gazetteers for research in Mississippi.

Peabody GNIS Service – Mississippi link to: http://peabody.research.yale.edu/cgi-bin/Query.GNIS?ST=Mississippi&SU=1

Color Landform Atlas – Mississippi link to: http://fermi.jhuapl.edu/states/ms_0.html

1985 U.S. Atlas link to: http://www.livgenmi.com/1895/MS/

Mississippi Hometown Locator link to: http://mississippi.hometownlocator.com/

Mississippi City Directories

City directories are similar to telephone directories in that they list the residents of a particular area. The difference though is what is important to genealogists, and that is they pre-date telephone directories. You can find an ancestor's information such as their street address, place of employment, occupation, or the name of their spouse. A one-stop-shop for finding city directories in Mississippi is the **Mississippi Online Historical Directories** which contains a listing of every available online historical directory related to Mississippi.

Mississippi Online Historical Directories:
https://sites.google.com/site/onlinedirectorysite/Home/usa/ms

Mississippi City Directories from 1860-1929 can be found at the **Library of Congress in Washington D.C.**

Library of Congress in Washington D.C.:
http://www.loc.gov/rr/microform/uscity/ms.html

Mississippi Genealogical Records

<u>Birth, Death, Marriage and Divorce Records</u> – Also known as vital records, birth, death, and marriage certificates are the most basic, yet most important records attached to your ancestor. The reason for their importance is that they not only place your ancestor in a specific place at a definite time, but potentially connect the individual to other relatives. Below is a list of repositories and websites where you can find Mississippi vital records.

Mississippi Vital records Office – birth and death records dating only from November 1912, Marriage from January 1, 1926 to June 30, 1938, and from January 1, 1942 to present, Divorce records from January 1, 1926 to June 30, 1938, and January 1, 1942 to present

Mississippi Vital Records
P.O. Box 1700
Jackson, MS 39215-1700
Tel: 601-576-7981

Mississippi Vital records Office:
http://msdh.ms.gov/msdhsite/_static/31,0,109.html

Mississippi Archives – microfiche copies of state death records from November 1912 to 1943, county marriage records, index of marriages before 1926, Freedman's Bureau marriage Index

William F. Winter Archives and History Building
200 North St.
Jackson, MS 39201
Tel: 601-576-6876
Fax: 601-576-6964

Mailing Address:

P.O. Box 571
Jackson, MS 39205-0571

Mississippi Archives:
http://mdah.state.ms.us/arrec/gen_research.php

Family Search has the following indexes which can be searched online for free:

Mississippi, Marriages, 1800-1911:
https://familysearch.org/search/collection/1680835

Mississippi, Tippah County Marriages, 1858-1979:
https://familysearch.org/search/collection/1916277

Census Reports

Census records are among the most important genealogical documents for placing your ancestor in a particular place at a specific time. Like BDM records, they can also lead you to other ancestors, particularly those who were living under the authority of the head of household.

Federal census records for Mississippi exist from 1820–1930 and can be found at:

Mississippi Archives – 1820–1930 federal population censuses, agricultural, manufacturing, and mortality schedules for 1850–80, slave schedules and indexes for 1850 and 1860, Dawes Rolls (Native American Enrollments), Enumeration of Educable Children

William F. Winter Archives and History Building
200 North St.
Jackson, MS 39201
Tel: 601-576-6876
Fax: 601-576-6964

Mailing Address:

P.O. Box 571
Jackson, MS 39205-0571

Mississippi Archives:
http://mdah.state.ms.us/arrec/gen_research.php

National Archives – Federal census Schedules for all states, 1790-1940

8601 Adelphi Road
College Park, MD 20740-6001
Tel: 1-866-272-6272

National Archives: http://www.archives.gov/research/census/

The **Free Census Project** has transcribed many Mississippi indexes and new material is added daily

Free Census Project: http://usgwcensus.org/cenfiles/ms.htm

Access Genealogy – Mississippi county census records from 1820-1930

Access Genealogy:
http://www.accessgenealogy.com/census/mississippi-census-records.htm

African American Census Schedules Online – slave schedules, mortality schedules, slave-owners census

African American Census Schedules Online:
http://www.afrigeneas.com/aacensus/ga/

Native Americans in Census Records (US National Archives)

Native Americans in Census Records:
http://www.archives.gov/research/census/native-americans/

Mississippi Church Records

Church and synagogue records are a valuable resource, especially for baptisms, marriages, and burials that took place before 1900. You will need to at least have an idea of your ancestor's religious denomination, and in most cases you will have to visit a brick and mortar establishment to view them.

Most church records are kept by the individual church, although in some denominations, records are placed in a regional archive or maintained at the diocesan level. Local Historical Societies are sometimes the repository for the state's older church records. Below are links archives that maintain church records, as well as a few databases that can be viewed online.

The **Family History Library** contains many church records from a variety of denominations on microfilm.

Family History Library:
http://familysearch.org/learn/wiki/en/Family_History_Library

Central Repositories for Denominational Records

Church of Jesus Christ of Latter-day Saints (Mormons)

Early Mormon Church records for Mississippi can be found on film located at the LDS Family History Library in Salt Lake City and can be searched via the **Family History Library Catalog**

Family History Library Catalog:
https://familysearch.org/eng/Library/FHLC/frameset_fhlc.asp

Mississippi Baptist Historical Collection
Mississippi College Library
200 S. Capitol Street
Clinton, MS 39060
Phone: (601) 925-3000

Mississippi Baptist Historical Collection:
http://library.mc.edu/resources/mississippi_baptist_historical_collect
ion/

Methodist

J.B. Cain Archives of Mississippi Methodism
Millsaps-Wilson Library
Millsaps College
1701 North State Street
Jackson, MS 39210
Phone: (601) 974-1073
Fax: (601) 974-1082

J.B. Cain Archives of Mississippi Methodismo:
http://www.millsaps.edu/library/library_cain_archives.php

Commission on Archives and History of the United Methodist Church
36 Madison Avenue
P.O. Box 127
Madison, NJ 07940
Phone: (201) 408-3590
Fax: (201) 408-3909

Commission on Archives and History of the United Methodist Church:
http://www.gcah.org/site/c.ghKJI0PHIoE/b.2858857/k.BF4D/Home.
htm

<u>Roman Catholic</u>

Diocese of Biloxi
1790 Popps Ferry Road
Biloxi, MS 39532
Phone: (228) 702-2100

Diocese of Biloxi: http://www.biloxidiocese.org/index.cfm

Diocese of Jackson
237 East Amite
P.O. Box 2248
Jackson, MS 39225
Phone: (601) 969-1880

Diocese of Jackson: http://www.jacksondiocese.org/catholic-dioces-archive.php

Mississippi Military Records

More than 40 million Americans have participated in some time of war service since America was colonized. The chance of finding your ancestor amongst those records is exceptionally high. Military records can even reveal individuals who never actually served, such as those who registered for the two World Wars but were never called to duty.

Below are a number of links to websites and archives that contain Mississippi military records.

Mississippi Archives – microfilm copies of service records for Mississippians in the War of 1812 (1812–15), Mexican War (1846–48), Civil War (1861–65), Spanish-American War (1898), draft registration cards for World War I (1917–18), Mississippi World War I statement of service cards, 1917–19

William F. Winter Archives and History Building
200 North St.
Jackson, MS 39201
Tel: 601-576-6876
Fax: 601-576-6964

Mailing Address:

P.O. Box 571
Jackson, MS 39205-0571

Mississippi Archives:
http://mdah.state.ms.us/arrec/gen_research.php

U.S. National Archives – WWI Draft registration cards, casualties lists, WWI and WWII service records, Korean War records, Vietnam War records, Civil War and Spanish-American War records, and casualties lists.

U.S. National Archives:
http://www.archives.gov/research/military/veterans/online.html

US Department of Veterans Affairs Nationwide Gravesite Locator – includes information on veterans and their family members buried in veterans and military cemeteries having a government grave marker.

US Department of Veterans Affairs Nationwide Gravesite Locator: http://gravelocator.cem.va.gov/

You may also find your ancestor's military records in the following databases:

United States General Index to Pension Files, 1861-1934: https://familysearch.org/search/collection/1919699

United States Index to Service Records, War with Spain, 1898: https://familysearch.org/search/collection/1919583

United States Index to Indian Wars Pension Files, 1892-1926 – military pension records of soldiers who fought in the Indian Wars between 1817 and 1898

United States Index to Indian Wars Pension Files, 1892-1926 link to: https://familysearch.org/search/collection/1979427

United States Registers of Enlistments in the U.S. Army, 1798-1914 - index of men who enlisted in the United States Army, 1798-1914.

United States Registers of Enlistments in the U.S. Army, 1798-1914: https://familysearch.org/search/collection/1880762

United States Mexican War Pension Index, 1887-1926 - index to Mexican War pension files for service between 1846 and 1848

United States Mexican War Pension Index, 1887-1926: https://familysearch.org/search/collection/1979390

Civil War Soldiers Service Records - Service records for both Union and Confederate soldiers indexed by soldier's name, rank, and unit.

Civil War Soldier Service Records:
http://go.fold3.com/civilwar_records/

Mississippi Cemetery Records

As convenient as it is to search cemetery records online, keep in mind that there are a few disadvantages over visiting a cemetery in person. They are:

- Tombstone information is not always accurately transcribed
- The arrangement of the graves in a cemetery can be crucial as family members are often buried next to each other or in the same grave. This arrangement is not always preserved in the alphabetical indexes that are found online.

With that information in mind, the following websites have databases that can be searched online for Mississippi Cemetery records.

Mississippi Tombstone Transcription Project - death and burial records

Mississippi Tombstone Transcription Project:
http://www.usgwtombstones.org/mississippi/

African American Cemeteries Online – African American, slave, and Native American cemetery records

African American Cemeteries Online:
http://africanamericancemeteries.com/ar/

Access Genealogy – huge database of Mississippi cemetery record transcriptions

Access Genealogy:
http://www.accessgenealogy.com/cemetery/mississippi-cemetery-records.htm

Find a Grave – over 100 million grave records can be searched on this site. Search can be conducted by name, location, or cemetery name.

Find a Grave: http://www.findagrave.com/

Interment.net - A free online database containing approximately 4 million cemetery records from around the world.

Interment.net: http://www.interment.net/

Billion Graves – as the name implies, you can search a billion records including headstone photos, transcriptions, cemetery records, and grave locations.

Billion Graves link to:
http://billiongraves.com/pages/search/index.php#cemetery

Mississippi Obituaries

Obituaries can reveal a wealth about our ancestor and other relatives. You can search our **Mississippi Newspaper Obituaries Listings** from hundreds of Mississippi newspapers online for free.

Mississippi Newspaper Obituaries Listings:
http://obituarieshelp.org/mississippi_newspaper_obituaries.html

Mississippi Wills and Probate Records

The documents found in a probate packet may include a complete inventory of a person's estate, newspaper entries, witness testimony, a copy of a will, list of debtors and creditors, names of executors or trustees, names of heirs. They can not only tell you about the ancestor you're currently researching, but lead to other ancestors.

Mississippi probate records have are kept by the chancery or probate courts. You can obtain copies of the records by contacting the **County Clerk's Office** in each county.

County Clerk's Office:
http://courts.ms.gov/trialcourts/circuitcourt/circuitclerks.pdf

Family Search has the following indexes that can be searched online for free:

Mississippi, Probate Records, 1781-1930:
https://familysearch.org/search/collection/2036959

Mississippi, Tippah County Records, 1836-1923:
https://familysearch.org/search/collection/1911456

Mississippi Immigration and Naturalization Records

The naturalization process generated many types of records, including petitions, declarations of intention, and oaths of allegiance. These records can provide family historians with information such as a person's birth date and place of birth, immigration year, marital status, spouse information, occupation, witnesses' names and addresses, and more.

Mississippi Archives - Index to Naturalization Records Mississippi Courts, 1798-1906

William F. Winter Archives and History Building
200 North St.
Jackson, MS 39201
Tel: 601-576-6876
Fax: 601-576-6964

Mailing Address:

P.O. Box 571
Jackson, MS 39205-0571

Mississippi Archives:
http://mdah.state.ms.us/arrec/gen_research.php

National Archives Southeast Region (Atlanta) –

5780 Jonesboro Road
Morrow, Georgia 30260
Tel: 770-968-2100
Fax: 770-968-2547

National Archives Southeast Region (Atlanta):
http://www.archives.gov/atlanta/

U.S. National Archives – Immigration and Naturalization records, 1787-1993

U.S. National Archives: http://www.archives.gov/research/guide-fed-records/groups/085.html

Mississippi Native American Records

Mississippi Archives –Dawes Rolls (Native American Enrollments)

William F. Winter Archives and History Building
200 North St.
Jackson, MS 39201
Tel: 601-576-6876
Fax: 601-576-6964

Mailing Address:

P.O. Box 571
Jackson, MS 39205-0571

Mississippi Archives:
http://mdah.state.ms.us/arrec/gen_research.php

Access Genealogy – Mississippi Native American census records, tribal histories, and much more

Access Genealogy :
http://www.accessgenealogy.com/native/mississippi-indian-tribes.htm

U.S. National Archives - information on American Indians who maintained their ties to Federally-recognized Tribes (1830-1970).

U.S. National Archives: http://www.archives.gov/research/native-americans/

Records of the Bureau of Indian Affairs (BIA)

Records of the Bureau of Indian Affairs (BIA):
http://www.archives.gov/research/guide-fed-records/groups/075.html

American Indians Records Repository - records dating from the 1700s including trust, education and other historic Indian Affairs records

American Indian Records Repository
Meritex Enterprises
17501 West 98th Street
Lenexa, KS 66219
Phone: 913-888-0601

American Indians Records Repository link to:
http://www.doi.gov/ost/records_mgmt/american-indian-records-repository.cfm

Missing Matriarchs – Resources for Researching Female Mississippi Ancestors

Looking for female ancestors requires an adjustment of how we view traditional records sources. A woman's identity was often under that of her husband, and often individual records for them can be difficult to locate. The following resources are effective in locating female ancestors in Mississippi where traditional records may not reveal them.

Bibliographies

1. *Something to Keep You Warm: The Roland Freeman Collection of Black American Quilts from the Mississippi Heartland,* Ronald L. Freeman (Mississippi Department of Archives and History, 1981)
2. *Mississippi Homespun: Nineteenth Century Textiles and the Women Who Made Them,* Mary Edna Lohrenz (Mississippi Department of Archives and History, 1989)

Selected Resources for Mississippi Women's History

Mississippi Historical Society
Po Box 571
Jackson, MS 39205-0571

University of Mississippi
Sarah Isom Center for Women's Studies
002 Lyceum
P.O. Box 1848
University, MS 38677
Tel: 662.915.5916
Email: isomctr@olemiss.edu

Common Mississippi Surnames

The following surnames are among the most common in Mississippi and are also being currently researched by other genealogists. If you find your surname here, there is a chance that some research has already been performed on your ancestor.

Adams, Alcorn, Amite, Attala, Benton, Bolivar, Calhoun, Carroll, Chickasaw, Choctaw, Claiborne, Clarke, Clay, Coahoma, Copiah, Covington, Desoto, Forrest, Franklin, George, Greene, Grenada, Hancock, Harrison, Hinds, Holmes, Humphreys, Issaquena, Itawamba, Jackson, Jasper, Jefferson, Jefferson, Jones, Kemper, Lafayette, Lamar, Lauderdale, Lawrence, Leake, Lee, Leflore, Lincoln, Lowndes, Madison, Marion, Marshall, Monroe, Montgomery, Neshoba, Newton, Noxubee, Oktibbeha, Panola, Pearl, Perry, Pike, Pontotoc, Prentiss, Quitman, Rankin, Scott, Sharkey, Simpson, Smith, Stone, Sunflower, Tallahatchie, Tate, Tippah, Tishomingo. Tunica, Union, Walthall, Warren, Washington, Wayne, Webster, Wilkinson, Winston, Yalobusha, Yazoo

About the Author

Gary L. Morris worked from 2009 to 2014 as a professional researcher for a major player in the genealogy field. After tracing his family lineage back to 1683, he has decided to publish these helpful guides to share the valuable information he has discovered during his career to help others trace their family lineages. An avid genealogist himself, he hopes you will find this guide factual, thorough, helpful, and most of all, effective in helping you to find your family members.